Personalisation: a rough guide

Sarah Carr

with Rachel Dittrich

First published in Great Britain in October 2008
by the Social Care Institute for Excellence

© SCIE 2008

ISBN 978-1-904812-45-6

Written by Sarah Carr (Social Care Institute for Excellence)

With Rachel Dittrich (Hampshire County Council Adult Services Department)

**This report is available in print and online
www.scie.org.uk**

Social Care Institute for Excellence
Goldings House
2 Hay's Lane
London SE1 2HB
tel 020 7089 6840
fax 020 7089 6841
textphone 020 7089 6893
www.scie.org.uk

Front cover image kindly supplied by Photofusion

This publication has no connection with Rough Guides Limited – the publisher of travel
guides and various non-reference titles based at 80 Strand, London WC2R 0RL.

Foreword

Personalisation means thinking about public services and social care in an entirely different way – starting with the person rather than the service. It will require the transformation of adult social care.

By identifying and transferring knowledge about good practice, SCIE has a special role to play in the transformation of social care services for adults. We are a signatory for the Putting People First concordat which set out our shared commitment to finding new ways to improve adult social care in England.

This new guide is intended to set out our current understanding of personalisation in its early stages as evidence emerges and problems are identified. SCIE aims to help the sector by rapidly absorbing lessons from innovations and pilots and by drawing on the experiences of early implementers and emerging research findings. This is the first of a series of publications designed to expand our knowledge about personalisation.

We have had help from a wide variety of people and hope that you find this guide a useful contribution to making personalisation a reality.

Julie Jones OBE
Chief Executive, SCIE

Acknowledgements

Special thanks to Richard Humphries for his invaluable expert advice and editorial input.

Thanks to all those who submitted practice examples, especially:

- Sara Lewis, Practice Development Manager, SCIE
- Mike Rudd, Project Support Officer, Strategic Development Unit, Adult and Community Services, Lancashire County Council
- Faith Dawes, Senior Communications Officer, Anchor Trust
- Jacqui London, Access Point Manager, Brighton and Hove City Council
- Karen Elsbury, Area Manager, Sense East.

Finally thanks to everyone at the SCIE Partners' Council and the personalisation project team who helped shape the initial idea for this guide.

Introduction

Photo: Photofusion

I just want to control my own life ... I like to socialise with other people and meet new friends. I just want to enjoy my freedom. I don't want people to control my life for me I want to control it myself. That's what my Mum brought me up for to control my own life. ('Maria' in Taylor and others, 2007, p 92)

Public service reform has proceeded far more successfully where government has successfully articulated a story about reform ... that has engaged the workforce. (Brooks, 2007, p 13)

This publication aims to tell the story so far about the personalisation of adult social care services. It is intended to be a 'rough guide', exploring what personalisation is, where the idea came from and placing the transformation of adult social care in the wider public service reform agenda. It explains some of the basics and examines what personalisation might mean for different social care stakeholders and for the sector as a whole.

Who the guide is aimed at

This guide is aimed at frontline practitioners and first-line managers in statutory and independent sector social care services.

How SCIE is trying to help

By identifying and transferring knowledge about good practice, SCIE has a special role to play in the transformation of social care services for adults. The organisation's priorities for 2008–11 will:

* support the transformation of social care services to enable people to lead full and independent lives
* support the delivery of services to transform the lives of families and their children
* raise the status of social care through a workforce that learns and innovates.

SCIE was a signatory of the *Putting people first* (HM Government, 2007) concordat, which set out the shared commitment to the transformation of adult social care in England.

SCIE recognises that the concept of personalisation continues to evolve in terms of both policy and practice. It intends to produce further materials to reflect emerging evidence and experience arising from implementation and further developments. This guide is not an effort to capture everything that is happening in personalisation, but rather offers a brief, accessible overview of some of the emerging ideas, issues and implications.

The basics

What is personalisation?

Personalisation means starting with the individual as a person with strengths and preferences who may have a network of support and resources, which can include family and friends. They may have their own funding sources or be eligible for state funding. Personalisation reinforces the idea the individual is best placed to know what they need and how those needs can be best met. It means that people can be responsible for themselves and can make their own decisions about what they require, but that they should also have information and support to enable them to do so. In this way services should respond to the individual instead of the person having to fit with the service. This traditional service-led approach has often meant that people have not received the right support for their circumstances or been able to help shape the kind of help they need. Personalisation is about giving people much more choice and control over their lives.

Personalisation itself is not necessarily a new idea – its origins will be explored later on in this section – nor is it just about giving people the option to have personal or individual budgets, although this is an important element. It applies to everyone with a whole range of needs, including those who may not be entitled to publicly funded care. Everyone needs universal access to information and advice to ensure they can choose the best support regardless of how their care is funded. All citizens should be able to access universal services such as transport, leisure and education facilities, housing, health services and opportunities for meaningful occupation.

Personalisation means:

- finding new collaborative ways of working and developing local partnerships, which produce a range of services for people to choose from and opportunities for social inclusion
- tailoring support to people's individual needs
- recognising and supporting carers in their role, while enabling them to maintain a life beyond their caring responsibilities
- a total system response so that universal and community services and resources are accessible to everyone
- early intervention and prevention so that people are supported early on and in a way that's right for them.

The Department of Health (DH) makes it clear that: 'Importantly, the ability to make choices about how people live their lives should not be restricted to those who live in their own homes. It is about better support, more tailored to individual choices and preferences in all care settings.' (DH, 2008a, p 5). This has equal, if not more, resonance for those living in residential care homes and other institutions, where personalised approaches may be less developed. Here, the independent sector has a crucial role to play in delivering personalised solutions for people no longer living in their own homes.

Personalisation is a relatively new term and there are different ideas about what it could mean and how it will work in practice. There are several terms used in association with personalisation or to describe services or activities that reflect the agenda. Some terms are used interchangeably and others are used in relation to particular policies, processes or people who use services. Based on our current understanding, the list below aims at clarifying some of the different examples of personalised approaches:

- **Person-centred planning** was an approach formally introduced in the 2001 *Valuing people* strategy (DH, 2001) for people with learning disabilities. The person-centred planning approach has similar aims and elements to personalisation, with a focus on supporting individuals to live as independently as possible, have choice and control over the services they use and to access both wider public and community services and employment and education. Rather than fitting people to services, services should fit the person.

Photo: Careimages.com

- **Person-centred care** has the same meaning as person-centred planning, but is more commonly used in the field of dementia care and services for older people.
- **Person-centred support** is a term being used by some service user groups to describe personalisation.
- **Independent living** is one of the goals of personalisation. It does not mean living on your own or doing things alone, but rather it means 'having choice and control over the assistance and/or equipment needed to go about your daily life; having equal access to housing, transport and mobility, health, employment and education and training opportunities' (Office for Disability Issues, 2008, p 11).
- **Self-directed support** is a term that originated with the in Control project and relates to a variety of approaches to creating personalised social care. in Control sees self-directed support as the route to achieving independent living. It says that the defining characteristics of self-directed support are:
  - The support is controlled by the individual.
  - The level of support is agreed in a fair, open and flexible way.
  - Any additional help needed to plan, specify and find support should be provided by people who are as close to the individual as possible.
  - The individual should control the financial resources for their support in a way they choose.

- All of the practices should be carried out in accordance with an agreed set of ethical principles. (Adapted from Duffy, 2008.)

This section addresses some of the questions that people have asked about the different approaches to delivering personalised social care.

What is a direct payment?

A direct payment is a means-tested cash payment made in the place of regular social service provision to an individual who has been assessed as needing support. Following a financial assessment, those eligible can choose to take a direct payment and arrange for their own support instead. The money included in a direct payment only applies to social services.

What is an individual budget?

Although they are just one way of approaching personalisation, much of the conversation about personalising services has focused on individual budgets (IBs). IBs have been piloted in 13 local authorities (Challis and others, 2007). Unlike direct payments, an IB sets an overall budget for a range of services, not just from social care, from which the individual may choose to receive as cash or services or a mixture of both.

IBs combine resources from the different funding streams to which an assessed individual is entitled. Currently, these are:

- local authority adult social care
- integrated community equipment services
- Disabled Facilities Grants
- Supporting People for housing-related support
- Access to Work
- Independent Living Fund.

Practice example: Direct payments for lesbian and gay people

The Commission for Social Care Inspection is issuing a series of equality and diversity bulletins designed to support providers in addressing the personalisation agenda in social care. The first bulletin looked at providing appropriate services for lesbian, gay, bisexual and transgender people and found that many people valued the choice and control direct payments gave them:

'I am a direct payments user. Yes, it has been a much better option for me as a gay person, no question. I would have been imprisoned with a care agency. Can't stress that too strongly. I live at home supported by people I recruit who I am very clear with who I am. They don't change every week and they are not all straight or gay ... life has been a thousand times better on direct payments, even with its challenges.'

'Staff treated me with respect because I was in control of who was employed and what they did to assist me, both in my home and the wider community. I would not employ someone who decided they would take over my life and decide what was best for me. And I certainly would not employ any person who did not feel comfortable around my lifestyle.'

The local authority is primarily responsible for ensuring an appropriate range of support is available for people who use services.

IBs aim to align assessments from the different funding streams, encourage self-assessment (where appropriate) and introduce transparent resource allocation systems (RAS), so an individual knows exactly what resources are included in their IB. IB holders are encouraged to devise support plans to help them meet desired outcomes and they can purchase support from social services, the private sector, voluntary or community groups or families and friends. Assistance with support planning may come from care managers, independent support planning/brokerage agencies, or family and friends.

IBs can be deployed in different ways:

- by the individual as a cash direct payment
- by the care manager
- by a trust
- as an indirect payment to a third party
- held by a service provider.

What is a personal budget?

Originally, the term personal budget only applied to social care funding but now it is often used interchangeably with individual budget. It is the funding given to someone after they have been assessed which should meet their needs. They can have the money as a direct payment or can choose to manage it in different ways. What is important is that these budgets give people a transparent allocation of money and the right to choose how this is managed and spent.

Where has personalisation come from?

Although the term personalisation is relatively recent, it has grown from a number of different ideas and influences that are summarised in this section.

Personalisation originates at least in part from **social work values**. Good social work practice has always involved putting the individual first; values such as respect for the individual and self-determination have long been at the heart of social work. In this sense the underlying philosophy of personalisation is familiar. The British Association of Social Workers (BASW) states that social work is committed to the five basic values of human dignity and worth; social justice; service to humanity, integrity and competence (BASW, 2002).

In terms of **public policy**, personalisation is not just about social care but is a central feature of the government's agenda for public sector reform. The Prime Minister's Strategy Unit report *Building on progress: Public services* (Prime Minister's Strategy Unit, 2007) described it as: 'the process by which services are tailored to the needs and preferences of citizens. The overall vision is that the state should empower citizens to shape their own lives and the services they receive' (p 33). Personalisation has become a key concept for the future of the NHS (DH, 2008d).

Its application to adult social care was announced in *Putting People first: A shared vision and commitment to the transformation of adult social care* (HM Government, 2007) – a ground-breaking concordat between central government, local government and the social care sector. This officially introduced the idea of a personalised adult social care system, where people will have maximum choice and control over the services they receive. It links to wider cross-government strategy including the notion of local authority 'place-shaping' (Lyons, 2007) and the local government White Paper *Strong and Prosperous Communities* (Department for Communities and Local Government, 2006).

The New Deal outlined in the 2008 Carers' Strategy has integrated and personalised services at its heart. Carers want recognition of their work and expertise, better service coordination, better information, improved joint working between staff and agencies, health and social care. Like Putting People First, the Carers' Strategy has been agreed by several government departments and was the result of a wide consultation. The shared vision is that by 2018 'carers will be universally recognised and valued as being fundamental to strong families and stable communities. Support will be tailored to meet individuals' needs, enabling carers to maintain a balance between their caring responsibilities and a life outside caring, whilst enabling the person they support to be a full and equal citizen' (HM Government, 2008, p 7).

Staying with public policy, personalisation can be seen as echoing many of the themes of the **community care reforms** that followed the National Health Service and Community Care Act 1990. The aim of these changes was to develop a needs-led approach, in which new arrangements for assessment and care management would lead to individuals receiving tailored packages of care instead of standard, block-contracted services.

In practical terms, a major impetus behind the development of individual or personal budgets has been the experience of **direct payments** that became available, initially to disabled adults of working age in England, as a result of the Community Care (Direct Payments) Act 1996, and have since been extended to other groups. The popularity and success of direct payments has stimulated much of the thinking around individual and personal budgets. As of March 2007, 54,000 people (including parents caring for disabled children and young carers) used direct payments (CSCI, 2008a).

Significantly, direct payments came about and were championed by disabled people themselves. The **service user movement** and the **social model of disability** have been powerful driving forces. Personalisation has some of its roots in the disability, mental health survivor and service user movements which emerged in 1970s, where individuals and groups undertook direct action and lobbied for change. Independent living, participation, control, choice and empowerment are key concepts for personalisation and they have their origins in the independent living movement and the social model of disability. The current personalisation policy has been influenced by the practical work of **in Control**, established as a social enterprise in 2003, which has pioneered the use of **self-directed support** and personal budgets as a way to reform the current social care system.

The initial phase of in Control's work was carried out across six local authorities from 2003 to 2005 and focused mainly on people with learning disabilities. It was positively evaluated and led on to a second phase which began to test the model for different people using social care (Poll and others, 2006). The whole evaluation collected information on 196 people in 17 English local authorities. The majority of people reported improvements to their lives since they began using self-directed support (Poll and Duffy, 2008). Now over 100 local authorities are looking towards the in Control self-directed support and individual budget model as a solution to delivering personalised social care services for all adults, and over 3,500 people are directing their own support.

Finally, personalisation has been shaped by the **policy thinking and ideas** of researchers, policy analysts and think tanks. One of the most significant contributors is Charles Leadbeater, whose influential Demos report *Personalisation through participation* (2004b) outlined a potential new script for public services. Drawing heavily on some of the influences highlighted above, he emphasises the direct participation of the people who use services: 'By putting users at the heart of services, by enabling them to become participants in the design and delivery, services will be more effective by mobilising millions of people as co-producers of the public goods they value' (Leadbeater, 2004b, p 19). He argues that personalised public services can have at least five different meanings:

- Providing people with customer-friendly versions of existing services.
- Giving people who use services more say in how they are run, once they have access to them.
- Giving people who use services a more direct say in how money is spent on services.
- Turning people who use services into co-designers and co-producers of services.
- Enabling self-organisation by society. (Leadbeater, 2004a, p 1)

The last two meanings are defined as 'deep personalisation', with people who use services working in equal partnership with providers. This is the type of personalisation that underpins social care transformation. It is not about modifying existing services, but changing whole systems and the way people work together.

Wider views of personalisation

Another term being used in discussions about personalisation is 'co-production'. Co-production is a fairly recent term that is used as a new way of talking about direct participation and community involvement in social care services in the UK. It has also been called 'co-creation' or 'parallel-production', and can be seen as a way of building social capital.

Practice example: Whole-system change
Hampshire County Council Commission of Inquiry into the future of services for adults in need of support and care

In response to Putting People First, the leader of Hampshire County Council launched a commission of inquiry to help shape future services for people in need of support and care. The commission has been gathering people's ideas, views and experiences in relation to the personalisation of adult social care, how social care can be funded and how it will change the relationship between the state, people who use services, their carers and families.

Through a series of hearings and round-table discussions, groups and individuals have been debating how the whole system can be changed to ensure that people are given more choice and control over the care they receive. Each hearing has focused on a theme. For each hearing all stakeholders were invited to submit their views in writing or any alternative format of their choice and experts were invited to present and discuss evidence. Experts include: people who use services and carers; partner organisations including government departments; service providers from all sectors; local authority representatives. The proceedings are published on Hampshire County Council's website. (http://www3.hants.gov.uk/adult-services/aboutas/consultation-involvement/commission-personalisation.htm)

Putting people first asserts that the transformation of adult social care programme 'seeks to be the first public service reform programme which is co-produced, co-developed, co-evaluated and recognises that real change will only be achieved through the participation of users and carers at every stage' (HM Government, 2007, p 1). In proposals for new ways of organising and delivering social care services, people who use services have suggested that 'service user-controlled organisations can be a site where social workers are employed working alongside service users in a hands-

on way' (Shaping Our Lives and others, 2007, p 13). This would seem to encapsulate the essence of co-production in adult social care.

Research on co-production has shown that frontline workers should focus on people's abilities rather than seeing them as problems (Boyle and others, 2006) and should have the right skills to do this. It has also said that developing staff confidence and improving how they feel about themselves and their jobs is very important. Co-production should mean more power and resources being shared with people on the front line – service users, carers and frontline workers – so they are empowered to co-produce their own solutions to the difficulties they are best placed to know about.

What does personalisation means for adult social care services?

> Personalisation is not a mechanism for public service reform. Rather, personalised services that meet the needs of the individual service user are one of they key objectives of such reforms. (Brooks, 2007, p 10)

This section discusses some of the emerging implications for:

- the social care workforce
- third sector organisations
- private sector providers
- service user organisations
- commissioning
- regulation.

Finally the key issues for social care sector as a whole are summarised.

The social care workforce

The role of social workers

In response to challenge of the personalisation agenda, the General Social Care Council (GSCC), along with partner agencies including SCIE, has examined social work roles and tasks for the 21st century. The GSCC states that integrated with these roles should be 'applying and extending the principles of personalisation, which have always been at the heart of social work at its best, to help people find individual solutions and achieve satisfactory outcomes' (GSCC, 2008a, p 15). It concluded that social work skills were critical to achieving the ambitions of the personalisation agenda, precisely because of the profession's core values and principles:

- a preventative approach
- the ability to work with complex situations and with different agencies and sectors
- the capacity to perform a wide range of tasks including brokerage and advocacy
- flexibility to step outside agency boundaries to serve people's best interests yet with the security of working in a regulated profession within a framework of law and regulation where people are accountable for their practice (GSCC, 2008a).

There has been some concern about the professional role of the social worker being undermined by the implications of creating more personalised services, but people have also argued that social work could have the opportunity to reaffirm and clarify its role. There is now the potential for social workers to move away from gatekeeping and resource management to advocacy and support tasks. A preliminary piece of research looking at the implications of self-directed support concluded that 'some social workers view the personalisation developments as an opportunity for them to return to the traditional social work role of enabling vulnerable people to achieve their potential. However, this is not what more recently qualified staff have been trained to do and competition for scarce social work skills is likely' (Henwood and Grove, 2006, pp 7–8). In other words, workers who have acquired skills that are more managerial in type may find transition to ways of working in personalised services, with self-assessment and self-directed support, more challenging.

People who use social care services and their carers consistently say:

People value a social work approach based on challenging the broader barriers they face. They place a particular value on a social approach, the social work relationship, and the positive personal qualities they associate with their social worker. These include warmth, respect, being non-judgmental, listening, treating people with equality, being trustworthy, open, honest and reliable and communicating well. People value the support that social workers offer as well as their ability to help them access and deal with other services and agencies (Shaping Our Lives, 2008).

Consistency and reliability have also been cited as especially important, along with the capacity for workers to keep their promises and go out of their way to help (Hopkins, 2007). The social work skills described here are those expected of social care practitioners in *Independence, well-being and choice*, which recognises that:

> people who use social care services say that the service is only as good as the person delivering it. They value social care practitioners who have a combination of the right human qualities as well as the necessary knowledge and skills. If we are to deliver our vision this means workers who are open, honest, warm, empathetic and respectful, who treat people using services with equity, are non-judgemental and challenge unfair discrimination. The workforce is therefore critical to delivery. (DH, 2005a, p 14).

Of people using self-directed support as part of the second in Control pilot, 71 per cent had help from a social worker (Poll and Duffy, 2008). *Making it personal* (Leadbeater and others, 2008, p 61) suggests that in a context of increasing self-directed support, social work roles will adapt accordingly and social workers could enjoy more creative, person-centred roles as:

- advisers: helping clients to self-assess their needs and plan for their future care
- navigators: helping clients find their way to the service they want
- brokers: helping clients assemble the right ingredients for their care package from a variety of sources
- service providers: deploying therapeutic and counselling skills directly with clients

- risk assessors and auditors: especially in complex cases and with vulnerable people deemed to be a risk to themselves or other people
- designers of social care systems as a whole: to help draw together formal, informal, voluntary and private sector providers.

As the last point suggests, social workers can also draw on their skills in counselling and community development to take forward personalisation. Here it is important to remember that personalisation is not only about individual budgets and self-directed support. 'There ... is a danger that assisting people with self-directed support could become the only and overriding definition of the social work role. Social work also has a contribution to make through its counselling competencies ... and has a tradition and track-record of community development, stimulating and supporting local community resources for disabled and older people' (Jones, 2008, p 46).

New types of working

In order to address the need for reaffirmation of some social work roles and for change in others, the Department of Health is developing an Adult Workforce Strategy which, as the Local Authority Circular states: 'will recognise that in developing a more personalised approach, it is essential that frontline staff, managers and other members of the workforce recognise the value of these changes, are actively engaged in designing and developing how it happens, and have the skills to deliver it' (DH, 2008, p 8). In statutory settings, some social work roles have become restricted by their 'control' function. The Skills for Care New Types of Worker programme is responding to some of these issues by exploring and developing what a new workforce will look like. The programme has been supporting pilot sites in England to explore workforce reform and trial new roles. In 2007 over 300 organisations took part in a mapping exercise which, among other things, identified personalisation as a key theme for workforce development. Skills for Care thinks new types of role might include:

- 'Hybrid roles' – this means, for example, social care workers or social workers doing tasks that have traditionally been done by other professionals such as workers from health, housing, justice, leisure, employment or other professions. It is any change to the way adult social care services are provided (or planned, commissioned or monitored) that aims to improve the lives of people using those services but is not yet available everywhere to everyone, or recognised as a 'mainstream' job, role or service.
- 'Person-centred working' – this means working in such a way that people who use services have as much control of their own lives as other people. This could be by making a person-centred plan or by using a direct payment or individual budget to arrange their own support and care, or to employ their own staff.
- 'Experts by experience' – people who have experience of using social care services or caring for people and who contribute to the 'business' of social care such as recruiting and training social care workers, assessing quality, commissioning services, planning changes to service delivery or regulation of services.
- Prevention and early intervention – workers supporting people early enough or in the right way, so that they don't need more intensive services. Types of provision might include support and modern equipment to stay at home, services provided in their community rather than in hospital, and support provided to keep people well and safe.
- Changes to organisations – to make them more effective, efficient and productive. For example, enabling workers to get their qualifications more quickly, working in partnership with other organisations and professions, integrating internally or externally or commissioning differently.
- Community support – supporting community networks so that people can be independent from services. (Adapted from Skills for Care, 2007, pp 1–2)

Social workers will need to be empowered by their organisations to in turn empower the people who are using the services, so organisational issues need to be considered. People who use social care services have recognised the limitations social workers can face when working within the constrained rules and resources of organisations (Beresford, 2007), but these do not always appear to be recognised in the various official documents. One of the current roles for social workers is to ration resources and identify priorities. This resource problem is unlikely to go away even if many more people are getting direct payments or have individual budgets (Blewett and others, 2007, p 25). While people who use services are clear that 'having a different relationship with social care staff is an important part of what they are seeking' (Blewett and others, 2007, p 28), they have been equally clear that the 'process of getting a service and the way in which it is delivered can have a major impact on users' experience of a service ... users did not perceive process as detached from outcome ...' (Shaping Our Lives and others, 2003, p 2). So people have indicated that

Practice example: Organisational change
Lancashire self-directed support service

In order to respond to the needs of a self-directed support system, some service providers in Lancashire have totally changed their recruitment and selection procedures, individually tailoring job specifications to each service user to ensure the best quality of care. Service users' budgets have also been given individual cost centre codes so that money can be identified rather than simply sit in one big pot.

Some provider organisations have extended learning disability training out beyond the usual frontline staff, all the way up to chief executive and director level. This creates a whole organisational awareness of personalisation issues that is not limited to frontline practitioners.

Informal use of personal budgets has allowed people to free up care hours. For example, one person used some funding to pay for someone to accompany them on holiday. This meant that no formal care hours were needed, which saved care hours and central funding.

although having greater choice of services may be a good thing, there also needs to be an improvement in how current services are provided, including addressing issues concerning budgets and rationing, along with the impact this has on the quality of social work. The National Consumer Council (NCC) recommends that 'where greater choice cannot create new efficiencies of scale or cost reduction, policy makers should be open and transparent about rationing decisions' (NCC, 2004, p 11).

Photo: Careimages.com

The role of social care staff

Making the social care personalisation agenda a reality has implications not just for social workers but for all frontline social care staff. Increasingly people will make arrangements with private individuals to provide the support they need, and this will raise a range of issues about employment rights, pay, health and safety and safeguarding. This already applies to people who make their own private arrangements for care in their own homes without recourse to public funding.

Recent attention has been paid to those employed directly by individuals to fulfil the role of personal assistants (PAs). A Skills for Care-commissioned study of direct payment employers and personal assistants found that 79 per cent of direct payment users were very satisfied with the support they receive from their directly employed PA, compared with 26 per cent who had been very satisfied with services supplied directly by the local authority. The study also showed that 95 per cent of PAs 'love their work'; 64 per cent were happy in their current role and many valued the flexible hours of the job (IFF Research, 2008). While this suggests that the direct payments system is working well for direct payment employers and PAs on an individual basis, the study also raises wider questions about the workforce such as pay, terms and conditions, training, registration and market capacity. These questions should be addressed ahead of the planned increase in uptake of direct payments and the spread of personal budgets.

The Skills for Care research also showed that one in three PAs considered themselves underpaid and that one in five thought they were required to work too many hours. The average hourly wage was found to be £7.60 an hour, with 8 per cent of employers paying less than £6 an hour. (The current national hourly minimum wage for adults over 22 is £5.73.) The research also found that 'the appropriateness and cost of training are an issue for direct payment employers, with only seven per cent of employers offering external training for PAs but a third of PAs wanting training and development for their role' (Skills for Care, 2008, p 1). These findings echo some concerns about the fact that PAs and homecare agency staff can work in conditions where they have little access to training, guaranteed holiday and sick pay, pensions or collective bargaining. It has been argued that people employing workers using direct payments (or personal budgets) 'need to be able to offer reasonable terms and conditions of employment to attract employees, and these workers deserve to be paid a fair wage' (Leece, 2007, p 195) so that 'user-controlled support does not founder on the inability of users to recruit and retain their personal assistants' (p 194).

Many other workers providing homecare support are employed by third sector or private agencies, which are rarely unionised or may have less favourable terms and conditions than the public sector (DH and Department for Education and Skills, 2006). The majority of those working in this sector are female, there are an increasing number of migrant workers in the field and staff turnover can be high (Experian, 2007; Eborall and Griffiths, 2008). Private sector employers argue that the pay and conditions of service they can offer their staff are constrained by what is affordable within the contract price set by public commissioners, and that policy expectations will not be delivered unless providers are funded realistically (ECCA, 2008).

Those planning, purchasing and providing personalised social care services need to be aware of the potential wider impact of certain associated workforce developments: 'Increasing user-controlled support may result in women losing jobs in the public sector where they have pension provision, union representation and safe working environments for casual employment as personal assistants with less beneficial terms and conditions' (Leece, 2007, p 194).

The Trades Union Congress (TUC) Commission on Vulnerable Employment's remit includes people who work for social care agencies or in care homes as being at risk of 'vulnerable employment' – that is, in precarious work where there may be an imbalance of power in the employer–worker relationship. The Commission warns that in certain low-paid sectors such as care, some employers may routinely break employment law and recommend that 'responsible employers should work together to challenge vulnerable employment' (TUC, 2008, p 5).

A report published by the Commission for Rural Communities says that 'the personalisation of social care will also have an effect on the social care workforce ... as many participants observed. Some were optimistic that new employment opportunities would emerge and saw this as a way to sustain local economies and communities. Others foresaw greater instability and disadvantages for care workers. Local authorities need to manage these risks with partner organisations and local needs assessments' (Manthorpe and Stephens, 2008, p 37). Workers with experience of working with older people in some rural budget pilot sites say they are concerned about travelling to remote areas, and the often isolated nature of their work (Manthorpe and Stephens, 2008).

At a strategic level, The DH's *Putting people first – Working to make it happen: Adult social care workforce strategy – interim statement* signals that 'the personalisation agenda will entail more sophisticated workforce planning which makes explicit links with other sectors. Such workforce planning must maximise opportunities for strategic market development, bring together skills across different professional groups, identify different ways of working and spell out the changing requirements within professional roles' (DH, 2008c, p 18).

Third sector organisations

The term 'third sector' is used to describe organisations that:

- are independent of the government
- work to achieve social, environmental and cultural aims
- mainly reinvest any profits they make to achieve those social, environmental or cultural aims.

The sector includes community groups, co-operatives and mutuals, voluntary groups, charities and social enterprises. (Adapted from HM Treasury, 2007, p 1)

Building on progress states that 'the Government should support the development of the many new and innovative services that provide tailored advice to specific community interest groups' (Prime Minister's Strategy Unit, 2007, p 42) and *Putting people first* makes it clear that a crucial part of developing personalised services is supporting third sector innovation, including social enterprise. *Independence, well-being and choice* says that 'local partners will need to recognise the diversity of their local population and ensure that there is a range of services, which meet the needs of all members of the local community' (DH, 2005a, p 12). In 2007 the Treasury issued its plans for the future role of the third sector in social and economic regeneration (HM Treasury, 2007), which stress the need for capacity-building and investment in the long-term future of the sector, which is seen as vital to transforming public services. Between 2008 and 2011 the third sector will receive £500m in government development money, ranging from direct grants to investment in sector research and skills strategies.

Clearly the third sector has a key part to play in the personalisation of social care services, having the potential to offer a wider choice of specific or specialist services, particularly for people from minority groups who have been historically underserved by generic statutory agencies: 'We recognise the role

Practice example: Independent living
Sense East's supported living project, Norfolk

A young woman who is deaf-blind and has a complex
syndrome with a deteriorating effect on both her mobility
and intellect was identified as needing support by the
outreach team. Her home life was becoming isolated and her
ageing parents were struggling to cope.

A supported living project was set up to enable the young
woman to live independently in the community. The complex
care team consulted her and her parents about what sort
of housing would best suit her needs and preferences. The
young woman decided on a town location and wanted a one-
bedroom ground-floor flat with no garden. The young woman,
her parents and Sense then explored what level of support
she needed and how this would take place, and a funding
package was set with the local authority. The package was
awarded to Sense with the full support of the young woman
and her family.

The young woman then participated in the selection of her
team and they supported her in equipping the flat, with
parental input as she directed. She has a personal finance
plan and is involved in planning her daytime activities. Her
evening funding is such that she has a staff team to take her
anywhere she chooses.

of third-sector organisations in representing the voices of different
groups and campaigning to achieve change for individuals and
communities' (HM Treasury, 2007, p 2). Strategic engagement with
this sector in social care may help to address some of the issues
with service provision and local diversity in certain areas. The
government is particularly keen to encourage the growth of third
sector providers as 'markets can challenge inefficiency – but the
'm' word raises fears of commercialisation and profit in services
funded by the taxpayer for some of society's most vulnerable

people. A community business that reinvests its surplus largely or entirely back into the business (and therefore the community) overcomes many such qualms' (Lorimer, 2008, p 1).

The Care Services Improvement Partnership (CSIP) define a social enterprise as 'a business that reinvests its surplus primarily back into the business for the interest of the community rather than working to make a profit for the benefit of shareholders alone' (Lorimer, 2008, p 12). The third sector, of which social enterprise is a part, is seen as important for delivering the diversity of provision to support the scope and type of choice required by the personalisation agenda. Local Area Agreements (LAAs) can be used to enable strategic planning and service delivery with the third sector and other community partners: 'Here, working with the third sector as a partner in the delivery of public sector services is a valuable approach, bringing with it flexibility, diversity and the potential to add value through contacts with additional revenue sources and increasing the social capital of communities. Many third sector organisations locally will also be uniquely placed to better support the hard-to-engage and disadvantaged groups within a community' (p 8). Such third sector partners should, for example, include user-led organisations. One particular area of provision that has the potential to be delivered through social enterprise is brokerage, information and advocacy services for people using individual budgets or direct payments: 'Personalisation support services facilitated by social enterprise are a valuable area for consideration, while commissioners may take longer to establish agreed strategic needs that will drive the shape of a wider, mixed economy of care' (p 16).

A Demos study has suggested that there will be positive impacts for the third sector from the increased use of personal budgets in social care, particularly as much of the innovation, advocacy and campaigning which resulted in the current wider social care reform had its roots in the work of social enterprise and voluntary organisations such as user-led Centres for Independent Living (Bartlett and Leadbeater, 2008). However, the authors warn that as the social care market develops, traditional third sector organisations will need to be mindful of the need to adapt and compete: 'Although the third sector has the right value base to thrive in a world of personal budgets, they might not always be as good at competing in the market – which may require branding, marketing and customer relationship management – as private sector providers' (p 5).

Private sector providers

Nearly half of all adult social care staff are employed by the private and voluntary sector and in many places they provide the majority of most services (CSCI, 2008a). Owners, managers and staff in the private sector thus have a crucial role to play in developing personalised solutions to people who use their services.

When direct payments were implemented, the Department of Health suggested that 'the greater use of direct payments and individualised budgets have the power to destabilise existing care markets' (DH, 2005c, p 27). Independent sector providers are becoming increasingly aware of this reality as the personalisation agenda is beginning to transform the way social care services are being conceived, commissioned and delivered. An increase in the use of self-directed support and personal budgets means there will be a smaller role for lengthy block-contracting and in-house service provision.

More generally, local authorities and partners will be looking to purchase different types of service from different sorts of provider. The aim is to foster greater choice and more flexible, responsive services to provide a more personalised service in both community and residential settings. It is likely that the projected changes are most likely to affect residential care home providers, day centres and domiciliary support services. However, there will almost certainly be a growth in the market for personal assistants and small-scale, flexible, specialist providers (Leece, 2007; Bartlett and Leadbeater, 2008) and for extra care housing, particularly for older people (Housing21, 2008).

For people in need of care and support, choice is only possible if the services they want to purchase are readily available, of good quality and have spare capacity to respond to choice. Local markets in many areas, particularly rural areas, still provide only limited choice to people. In the case of residential care, the

Photo: Photofusion

'cartelization of the market' by a small number of large corporate providers means that being given an individual budget may be of little significance, as the consumer has an increasingly limited choice of provider' (Dittrich, 2008). Thus local authorities have been asked to develop and shape the market to ensure sufficient provision for enabling choice. This means reforming how services are commissioned and procured.

To develop services that are focused on the person, and are competitive within a social care market geared towards personalisation, private sector providers can learn from what their customers have been saying and what the personalisation policy aims at achieving. As Bartlett and Leadbeater note: 'While the private sector care services offer more flexible hours, its services can also be too impersonal. Care depends on intimacy and relationships – it is not just a transaction, but on a relationship of trust between carer and cared for. The contracted-out care services market often fails to deliver such relationships, for example they have a very high staff turnover, which service users consistently complain about' (Bartlett and Leadbeater, 2008, p 18). So private providers need to ask whether they are able to respond to the demand for individually tailored services based

Practice example: Personalisation in a residential setting
Anchor Homes' food ordering system

Anchor Homes is the largest not-for-profit provider of residential and nursing care in the sector. In 2006 they began piloting a new meal ordering system in their care homes. Previously residents had to order their food a day or more in advance, as was the case in most care homes. However, under the new system residents are able to choose what they want as they sit down to eat. Now they can choose based on seeing and smelling the food.

This more personalised approach to mealtimes means that staff don't have to spend hours collecting food orders in advance and are freer to provide care and support. Now residents are making decisions based on what they like the look and smell of, they are eating more and less is wasted. Any savings go back into buying even better food.

Residents are more adventurous in their food choices. The chefs regularly hold meetings and gather feedback from residents on meal choices and are guided by residents' requests and favourite recipes. If what's on offer doesn't appeal to someone, chef managers can still make a simple alternative if that's what the individual would prefer.

on good, stable relationships between staff and people using services. Equally, local authorities should work with providers to help with predicting how the market might change and encourage innovation (Manthorpe and Stephens, 2008). A new, more trusting relationship is required between commissioner and provider. This should be based on achieving the right outcomes for the individual, their carers and community rather than financial concerns: 'at present service providers are kept at arm's length from the detailed planning process, because they are perceived as tending to drive up costs in order to meet their own needs' (Bartlett and Leadbeater, 2008, p 28). The concerns of many providers that personalisation and other policy expectations will not be delivered unless accompanied by realistic public funding have already been noted.

User-led organisations

It is important to recognise that personalisation is not about individualisation *per se* but represents a broader, more varied approach. The potential for personalisation to encompass collective ways of working has been articulated by Iain Ferguson:

> A sense of powerlessness ... affects not only those who use health and social services, but also those who work in them. Overcoming that sense of powerlessness, however, will involve moving beyond individualism and the market-based solutions of personalisation theory. It will require the development and strengthening of *collective* organisation both amongst those who use services and amongst those who provide them. One of the most exciting and challenging developments in social work and social care over the past twenty years – Independent Living Centres [sic], advocacy schemes, new models of crisis services and, above all, social models of disability and mental health – have emerged out of the collective experience and organisation of service users. (Ferguson, 2007, p 401).

Some have argued that highly individualised approaches may undermine collective social care initiatives and opportunities for developing cooperative organisations led by those using services, or peer advocacy. One report concerning the implementation of self-directed support and individual budgets identified the loss of collectivism 'where there is an apparent tension between the emphasis on the individual rather than on collective objectives' (Henwood and Grove, 2006, p ii) as an ideological obstacle to reform. The Institute for Public Policy Research (IPPR) has stated that individual choice is best supported by 'having forms of collective voice and influence, peer support and accountability of providers to users ... [but] routes for collective influence are currently lacking, as are spaces in which to engage with and support each other' (Moullin, 2008, p 5), while the New Economics Foundation (NEF) argues that 'individual budgets without mutual support misunderstand the nature of public services' (NEF, 2008, p 15).

IPPR has recommended that 'mechanisms for exercising collective voice should be focused on larger and more significant decisions and priority-setting exercises, and be better resourced' (Brooks, 2007, p 9). *Putting people first* makes it clear that as part of system-wide transformation there should be 'support for at least one local user led organisation and mainstream mechanisms to develop networks which ensure people using services and their families have a collective voice, influencing policy and provision' (HM Government, 2007, p 4). The Improving life chances of disabled people strategy of 2005 (Prime Minister's Strategy Unit, 2005) included the expansion of Centres for Independent Living to support, advise and advocate for disabled people. The direct

Practice example: A user-led organisation
Essex Coalition of Disabled People

Essex Coalition of Disabled People (ECDP) is an organisation run by and for disabled people in Essex and its environs. It is funded both by the council and charitable trusts. Its main aim is to enhance the quality of the lives of disabled people in Essex who have physical and sensory impairments, learning difficulties and/or who are mental health system survivors. ECDP seeks to increase opportunities for disabled people, whether these are within the working environment, or are social and leisure opportunities.

The organisation is actively involved with the county's health and social care decision-makers and service providers. It provides a criminal records bureau checking service, direct payments support services, volunteer and mentoring opportunities, a personal assistant register and professional training. (www.ecdp.org.uk)

Photo: Photofusion

involvement of disabled people through Centres for Independent
Living was seen as one of the key ingredients to the Life chances
programme and is now understood as a vital component of wider
social care transformation. The National Centre for Independent
Living (NCIL) and the Association of Directors of Adult Social
Services (ADASS) have a joint protocol for the provision of centres
for independent living and user-led support services (NCIL/ADASS,
2006).

There is an expectation that councils will talk directly to
disabled people and their organisations in order to implement
system change, but this assumes that those user-led organisations
exist and have the capacity to undertake their new and expanded
roles. In 2006 the DH commissioned a research study into the
role and capacity of user-led organisations. The national mapping
exercise showed that 'the existence of local user-led organisations
is inconsistent and patchy. Analysis of the data indicates that in
the majority of localities (98 per cent) there are 15 or less user-
led organisations. In some areas (18 localities or 12 per cent) no
user-led organisations were identified at all, while in a substantial
number only one to five user-led organisations were found
(76 localities or 51 per cent)' (Maynard Campbell, 2007, p 5).

Therefore, development work urgently needs to happen if user-led organisations are to have as powerful and influential a role as they should.

The cross-government Independent Living Strategy (Office of Disability Issues, 2008) includes an investment in the development of 12 user-led organisations as action and learning sites to

Practice example: Strategic commissioning
'Sustainable commissioning' in Camden

The Camden commissioning project, which has been funded through the Treasury 'Invest to Save' budget, aims to improve the way public services are commissioned so that the wider social, economic and environmental impacts of services are taken into account. The project is piloting the New Economics Foundation's Sustainable Commissioning Model to look again at the provision of day services for people with mental health problems. The winner of the tender to provide new day services in mental health was a consortium of local organisations including MIND in Camden, Holy Cross Centre Trust and Camden Volunteer Bureau. The consortium was not the cheapest tender on a unit cost basis, but commissioners felt their focus on wider social and economic impacts would create the most positive outcome for the whole community.

The Sustainable Commissioning Model contains two key elements:

1. An **Outcomes Framework** to ensure social, economic and environmental impacts are accounted for in the tendering process and delivery. The framework encourages innovation by allowing providers to explain how their activities and outputs will achieve certain service level and wider outcomes, as identified by the local authority.
2. A **Valuing Model** which tracks social, environmental and economic outcomes and includes a financial savings component. (www.procurementcupboard.org)

promote service improvement, mentoring between organisations and to share learning to foster the development of user-led organisations in general. However, it will be up to local authorities to support user-led organisations as partners because 'the success of [the] whole system change is predicated on engagement with communities and their ownership of the agenda at local level' (DH, 2008a, p 9). A critical success factor for user-led organisation development 'appeared to be how user-led organisations are perceived and supported within the local authority environment; such as where they fit in to local spending priorities; whether the idea of nurturing a strong user voice is seen as important or "difficult"; or whether it is down to one or two individuals who have reason to champion the cause' (Maynard Campbell, 2007, p 8). As part of their personalisation strategies, local authorities will need to commit to resourcing user-led organisations and to recognise them as equal partners in Local Area Agreements rather than optional extra or tokenistic consultants (Bennett, 2008): 'The value of services provided by service user organisations needs to be written into service level agreements. If services are run by service user organisations they could bring health and social care together' (Shaping Our Lives and others, 2007, p 13).

Commissioning

Commissioning has been defined by the Commission for Social Care Inspection (CSCI) as 'the process of translating aspirations into timely and quality services for users which meet their needs; promote their independence; provide choice; are cost effective; and support the whole community' (CSCI, 2006, p 5). The vision for NHS world-class commissioning states that the activity is more about transformation than transaction (DH, 2007a) and the NHS Institute for Innovation and Improvement (NHS Institute) has issued a guide for health and social care commissioners designed to promote services innovation (NHS Institute, 2008). Lord Darzi's *NHS next stage review final report* says that 'every primary care trust will commission comprehensive wellbeing and prevention services, in partnership with local authorities, with services offered personalised to meet the specific needs of their local populations'

(DH, 2008d, p 9). This approach is already underpinned by joint strategic needs assessments, where primary care trusts and local authorities are expected to produce strategies for the health and wellbeing of their local community.

Following *Putting people first* (HM Government, 2007), by 2011 all councils will be expected to have: 'a commissioning strategy which includes incentives to stimulate development of high quality services that treat people with dignity and maximise choice and control as well as balancing investment in prevention, early intervention/reablement and providing intensive care and support for those with high-level complex needs. This should have the capacity to support third/private sector innovation, including social enterprise and where appropriate undertaken jointly with the NHS and other statutory agencies such as the Learning and Skills Council' (DH, 2008a, p 24).

Local authorities are now being encouraged to change from thinking about service commissioning to thinking about strategic investment: 'Directors of Adult Social Services will need to consider making some long term investments in innovative services that users are starting to request.... Commissioners need to become what some have termed "strategic bridge builders" meaning they look for gaps in the market for services people seem to be demanding and use strategic investments to encourage this market to develop' (Bartlett and Leadbeater, 2008, p 29).

The notion that commissioning needs to change if personalisation is to become a reality has been stressed (CSCI, 2006) and directions on how this might be achieved have been gradually emerging. In its framework for commissioning, CSIP stresses the need for a balance between a focus on market-shaping and other commissioning issues relating to personal budgets and building on the broader agenda of commissioning for the health and well-being of all citizens so that the benefits of personalisation can be felt by everyone: 'All people are dependent on social networks, universal services and the resources of communities in which they live to become active citizens. This logically leads to the consideration of an inclusive approach to commissioning – that is about shaping the places in which we live and supporting everyone to live better lives' (Bennett, 2008, p 13). CSIP offers a model of multi-level commissioning that includes:

- Strategic – area-wide and regional-level joint commissioning with a three- to ten-year outlook. Working across whole community to develop the local market to support personalisation, to develop the workforce and to ensure that universal public services are accessible to all.
- Operational – locality-based commissioning and support to citizens commissioning. Day-to-day commissioning activities with a one- to two-year outlook. Working to support citizens in directing their own care with information, advocacy, brokerage and training.
- Citizen – citizens directing their own support, personal and individual budget holders.

Practice example: Information and advice
Brighton and Hove Access Point

The Access Point is the adult social care contact centre for Brighton and Hove. It provides a point of access for adults wishing to access social care services or who require advice and information in order to access services independently.

The Access Point brings together the Older People's Community Assessment team, the Physical Disability (under 65) Assessment team, the Sensory team, Occupational Therapy and the Learning Disability team. By contacting the centre by phone, minicom, e-mail or fax, the person using the service can access information on or assessment for any one or more of these services. Traditionally each of these services had its own contact number and would complete its own initial assessment, meaning that people who required more than one service or advice and information from a variety of services would need to call various numbers and undergo a number of assessments. The Access Point ensures more accessible services, and needs- as opposed to service-led assessment.

Photo: Photofusion

Regulation

Overview

The shift towards person-centred services raises questions about the role and functions of regulatory bodies and systems. The government is tackling some of the issues in its Better Regulation programme of work, which is looking at risk and responsibility in public services. Social care has inherited a regulation and inspection system focused on the regulator and the services rather than the person using the services, their carers and families. A regulation and inspection system needs to ensure that policies and procedures provide assurance around quality and safety, as well as focus on better outcomes for people (Fraser, 2008). The DH has undertaken a consultation on the framework for the registration of health and adult social care providers (DH, 2008b). It puts the emphasis on public safety and quality. It noted that people increasingly exercise choice as to how, when and where they receive their care and thus influence the development of more flexible, responsive and convenient high-quality services from their providers.

Personalisation is likely to require new, more flexible approaches to regulation, able to adapt to innovative support from new types of providers offering broader opportunities including scope for people to take appropriate risks. It will also be important to establish close working links between the regulator, the Director of Adult Social Services with a remit for market development and quality assurance, and local adult protection services. CSCI has responded to the challenges of personalisation by starting its Experts by Experience inspection programme, where people who use services have a direct role as inspectors. The Commission's assessment of council services in 2007/08 is taking into account the Putting People First agenda, considering how personalisation policies are being applied in communities, building on the outcomes of the previous framework, *Our health, our care, our say* (DH, 2006). The assessments will include new performance measures and inspection methods appropriate to personalisation (CSCI, 2008b). When CSCI merges with the Mental Health Act Commission and the Healthcare Commission in 2009 to become the new Care Quality Commission, it is expected that such person-centred regulatory approaches, which empower both the people who use services, and their carers and families, will become standard practice.

Workforce regulation

The General Social Care Council (GSCC) is assessing if there is support for the regulation of personal assistants (PAs). The key principles that will shape their approach are:

- any register must add value to the experience of people employing their own PAs
- it must enable people to make informed choices when employing a PA who is a friend or family member
- the form of regulation must fit with the new freedoms and flexibilities granted to people under the personalisation agenda. (Adapted from GSCC, 2008b.)

Safeguarding is an aspect of regulation that is of concern to social care stakeholders implementing approaches to service delivery that increase choice and control. The initial findings from the individual budget (IB) pilot site evaluation concluded that local authority adult protection leads can have unique insights from working at the intersection between the demand for safety for the individual, assurances about spending public money and the increased demand for choice and control in social care. The researchers recommend that their expertise is used consistently with IB implementation, with safeguarding issues being addressed at an early stage (Manthorpe and others, 2008).

CSCI recognises that 'it is important not to be over-protective or prevent adults from leading ordinary lives – but this must be weighed against individuals' fundamental right to expect to be safe and to be protected and safeguarded from harm' (CSCI, 2008c, p 11). It emphasises the need for clarity for roles and responsibilities of agencies involved in safeguarding adults (within social care and wider public services) with clearer definitions of what constitutes abuse and harm. The Department of Health's *Independence, choice and risk: A guide to best practice in supported decision-making* recognises the complexities involved in managing risk in relation to choice. However, the guide is clear that 'ultimately, the local authority has a statutory duty of care and a responsibility not to agree to support a care plan if there are serious concerns that it will not meet an individual's needs or if it places an individual in a dangerous situation' (DH, 2007b, p 2).

What are the key issues for the social care sector as a whole?

The personalised social care system will need to meet a number of set objectives:

- a universal information, advice and advocacy service for people needing services and their carers, including those funding their own care
- person-centred planning and self-directed support becoming mainstream

- a fair and transparent system for allocating resources to people with different levels of need
- personal budgets as an option for everyone eligible for publicly funded support
- an increase in the take-up of direct payments
- family members, friends and carers to be treated as experts and supported in their role as well as having a life outside their caring responsibilities
- commissioning processes that encourage services offering high standards of care, dignity and maximum choice and control
- a common assessment process with greater emphasis on self-assessment
- ensuring people, their carers and families have a collective voice, influencing policy and provision
- adult social care services championing the rights and needs of people across the local authority, public services and the wider community
- the promotion of dignity in local care services as part of systems aiming to minimise the risk of abuse and neglect of vulnerable adults
- prevention, early intervention and re-ablement as more standard practice
- supporting people to remain in their own homes as long as possible while combating potential isolation
- viewing telecare as integral rather than marginal.

The personalised system will need to be cost-effective and sustainable in the long term. When the Government develops the reform strategy for the long-term funding of care, the system will need to be affordable and be consistent with principles of fairness and universalism. This means the transformation towards personalisation must consider:

- The changing population and associated rising demand. It is a mark of progress that people are living longer, but this does mean more demand for services, including from people living longer in ill-health.

- How to meet the requirements for further efficiencies and continued outcome and performance improvement.
- Approaches to eligibility. In its State of Social Care report for 2006–07 (CSCI, 2008a), the Commission criticised councils for tightening their eligibility criteria. There is an increasingly sharp divide between those people who qualify for the formal system of social care and those who are outside it. People who are not eligible for council-arranged services and cannot purchase their care independently often struggle with poor information, fragile informal support arrangements and a poorer quality of life.
- What a new way of funding care might look like and which elements will be universal.
- Looking at how to manage and pool different funding streams and resources including those from social care, health, the NHS, welfare benefits and people's own contributions.
- What contract to develop between the state, individuals, families and communities, including rights and responsibilities on both sides.

4

Conclusion

> Person-centred support is not another thing services have to do; it's what they must do. It's not another job – it's *the* job (Glynn and others, 2008, p 11).

Personalisation means thinking about public services and social care in an entirely different way – starting with the person rather than the service. Although this shift will take time, it will ultimately mean change at every level throughout the whole local authority system to ensure that universal services such as transport, housing and education are accessible to all citizens. This means that commissioning must change to be more strategic and open with a focus on the local community, its resources and the people who use the services. Approaches to early intervention and prevention need to develop further so that people are encouraged to stay healthy and independent.

In social care total organisational and cultural change will need to take place so that people, rather than systems and procedures, come first. This will include fostering innovative and collaborative ways of working, giving universal access to information and advice to everyone in need of support regardless of where their funding comes from. It will also require supporting social care practitioners to work in new ways alongside people who use services, their carers, families and communities.

This guide is intended to sketch out our current understanding of personalisation at this very early stage of implementation. SCIE aims to support the sector by rapidly absorbing lessons from innovations and pilots, drawing on the experiences of early implementers and emerging research findings, and making these accessible through further products and initiatives.

Further information

For more on personalisation

The Social Care Institute for Excellence
www.scie.org.uk

For more information on how direct payments work please see SCIE's *Resource Guide 5: Direct Payments: Answering Frequently Asked Questions*, which was produced with the National Centre for Independent Living (NCIL).

For more information on how direct payments are working for black and minority ethnic people please see SCIE's *Race Equality Position Paper 1: Will Community-Based Support Services Make Direct Payments a Viable Option for Black and Minority Ethnic Service Users and Carers?*

For more about the role of people who use services in culture change see *SCIE People Management Knowledge Review 17: Developing Social Care: Service Users Driving Culture Change*, produced by Shaping Our Lives, National Centre for Independent Living and University of Leeds Centre for Disability Studies.

Social Care Online
www.scie-socialcareonline.org.uk

Care Services Improvement Partnership Personalisation Network
www.integratedcarenetwork.gov.uk/Personalisation

Care Services Improvement Partnership personalisation toolkit
www.integratedcarenetwork.gov.uk/Personalisation/
PersonalisationToolkit

Department of Health personalisation web pages
www.dh.gov.uk/en/SocialCare/Socialcarereform/Personalisation/
index.htm

in Control
www.in-control.org.uk

Hampshire County Council personalisation briefings
www3.hants.gov.uk/adult-services/aboutas/consultation-
involvement/commission-personalisation/personalisation-
commissioners-briefings.htm

**The IBSEN project – National evaluation of the Individual
Budgets Pilot Projects**
http://php.york.ac.uk/inst/spru/research/summs/ibsen.php

For general information on social care transformation

Commission for Social Care Inspection (CSCI)
www.csci.org.uk

General Social Care Council (GSCC)
www.gscc.org.uk

Skills for Care
www.skillsforcare.org.uk

Office for Disability Issues
www.officefordisability.gov.uk

Office of the Third Sector
www.cabinetoffice.gov.uk/third_sector.aspx

Demos
www.demos.co.uk

Institute for Public Policy Research (IPPR)
www.ippr.org

Association of Directors of Adult Social Services (ADASS)
www.adss.org.uk

British Association of Social Workers
www.basw.co.uk

Shaping Our Lives National User Network
www.shapingourlives.org.uk

National Centre for Independent Living
www.ncil.org.uk

English Community Care Association (ECCA)
www.ecca.org.uk

References

Bartlett, J. and Leadbeater, C. (2008) *Personal budgets: The impact on the third sector*, London: Demos.

BASW (British Association of Social Workers) (2002) *The code of ethics for social work*, Birmingham: BASW.

Bennett, M. (2008) *Commissioning for personalisation: A framework for local authority commissioners*, London: Care Services Improvement Partnership/Department of Health.

Beresford, P. (2007) *The changing roles and tasks of social work from service users' perspectives: A literature-informed discussion paper*, London: Shaping Our Lives National User Network.

Blewett, J., Lewis, J. and Tunstill, J. (2007) *The changing roles and tasks of social work: A literature-informed discussion paper*, London: General Social Care Council.

Boyle, D., Clark, S. and Burns, S. (2006) *Co-production by people outside paid employment*, York: Joseph Rowntree Foundation.

Brooks, R. (ed) (2007) *Public services at the crossroads: Executive summary*, London: Institute for Public Policy Research.

Challis, D. and others (2007) *Individual budgets evaluation: A summary of early findings*, York: University of York Social Policy Research Unit, available at www.york.ac.uk/inst/spru/pubs/rworks/IbsenSummary.pdf

CSCI (Commission for Social Care Inspection) (2006) *Relentless optimism: Creative commissioning for personalised care*, London, CSCI.

CSCI (2008a) *State of social care in England 2006–2007*, London: CSCI.

CSCI (2008b) *CSCI Annual report 2007–2008,* London: The Stationery Office.

CSCI (2008c) *Raising voices: Views on safeguarding adults*, London: CSCI.

Department for Communities and Local Government (2006) *Strong and prosperous communities*, London: HMSO.

DH (Department of Health) (2001) *Valuing people: A new strategy for learning disability for the 21st century*, London: The Stationery Office.

DH (2005a) *Independence, well-being and choice: Our vision for the future of social care for adults in England*, London: DH.

DH (2005c) *Health reform in England: Update and next steps*, London: DH.

DH (2006) *Our health, our care, our say: A new direction for community services*, London: DH.

DH (2007a) *World class commissioning: Vision*, London: DH.

DH (2007b) *Independence, choice and risk: A guide to best practice in supported decision-making – Executive summary*, London: DH.

DH (2008a) *Local authority circular LAC (DH)(2008)1: Transforming social care*, London: DH.

DH (2008b) *The future regulation of health and adult social care in England: A consultation on the framework for the registration of health and adult social care providers*, London: DH.

DH (2008c) *Putting people first – working to make it happen: Adult social care workforce strategy – interim statement*, London: DH.

DH (2008d) *High quality care for all: NHS next stage review final report*, London: DH

DH and Department for Education and Skills (2006) *Options for excellence: Building the social care workforce of the future*, London: DH.

Dittrich, R. (2008) *Putting people first briefing paper 7: The care market – summary of pre-existing evidence from experts and research*, available at http://www3.hants.gov.uk/briefingpaper7-2.pdf

Duffy, S. (2008) *in Control mythbuster and frequently asked questions*, Birmingham: in Control publications.

Eborall, C. and Griffiths, R. (2008) *The state of the adult social care workforce in England 2008: The third report of Skills for Care's skills research and intelligence unit*, Leeds: Skills for Care.

ECCA (English Community Care Association) (2008) *Nothing for services, nothing for quality*, London: ECCA.

Experian (2007) *Overseas workers in the UK social care, children and young people sector: A report for Skills for Care and Development*, London: Skills for Care and Development.

Ferguson, I. (2007) 'Increasing user choice or privatising risk? The antimonies of personalisation', *British Journal of Social Work*, vol 37, pp 387–403.

Fraser, J. (2008) *Personalisation and regulation*, CSCI presentation to SCIE independent sector seminar on personalisation 15 July 2008, unpublished.

Glynn, M. and others (2008) *Person-centred support: What service users and practitioners Say*, York: Joseph Rowntree Foundation.

GSCC (General Social Care Council) (2008a) *Social work at its best: A statement of social work roles and tasks for the 21st Century*, London: GSCC.

GSCC (2008b) *Media release 30/06/08: Consultation announced on the regulation of personal assistants*, London: GSCC.

Henwood, M. and Grove, B. (2006) *Here to Stay? Self-directed support: Aspiration and implementation – A review for the Department of Health*, Towcester: Melanie Henwood Associates.

HM Government (2007) *Putting people first: A shared vision and commitment to the transformation of adult social care*, London: HM Government.

HM Government (2008) *Carers at the heart of 21st century families and communities: A caring system on your side, A life of your own*, London: HM Government.

HM Treasury (2007) *The future role of the third sector in social and economic regeneration*, London: Cabinet Office.

Hopkins, A. (2007) *Delivering public services: A report to the Office of the Third Sector by the National Consumer Council*, London: National Consumer Council.

Housing21 (2008) *'Building choices': Personal budgets and older people's housing – broadening the debate: Report,* London: Housing Corporation/CSIP.

IFF Research (2008) *Employment aspects and workforce implications of direct payment*, Leeds: Skills for Care.

Jones, R. (2008) 'Self-directed support: watching for the pitfalls', *Journal of Integrated Care*, vol 16, no 1, pp 44–7.

Leadbeater, C. (2004a) *A Summary of 'Personalisation through participation: A new script for public services'*, London: Demos.

Leadbeater, C. (2004b) *Personalisation through participation: A new script for public services*, London: Demos.

Leadbeater, C., Bartlett, J. and Gallagher, N. (2008) *Making it personal*, London: Demos.

Leece, J. (2007) 'Direct payments and user-controlled support: the challenges for social care commissioning', *Practice*, vol 19, no 3, pp 185–98.

Lorimer, R. (2008) *Integration for social enterprise,* London: CSIP Integrated Care Network.

Lyons, M. (2007) *Lyons inquiry into local government: Place shaping – a shared ambition for the future of local government*, London: The Stationery Office.

Manthorpe, J. and Stephens, M. (2008) *The personalisation of adult social care in rural areas*, Cheltenham: Commission for Rural Communities.

Manthorpe, J. and others (2008) 'Safeguarding and system change: early perceptions of the implications for adult protection services of the English individual budgets pilots: a qualitative study', *British Journal of Social Work Advance Access*, 17 March 2008.

Maynard Campbell, S. (2007) *Mapping the capacity and potential for user-led organisations in England*, London: DH.

Moullin, S. (2008) *Just care? A fresh approach to adult services*, London: Institute for Public Policy Research.

NCC (National Consumer Council) (2004) *Making public services personal*, London: NCC.

NCIL/ADASS (2006) Joint protocol between National Centre for Independent Living (NCIL) and Association of Directors of Social Services (ADASS) for the provision of Centres for Independent Living (CILs) and user-led support services, London: NCIL/ADASS.

NEF (New Economics Foundation) (2008) *Co-production: A manifesto for growing the core economy*, London: NEF.

NHS Institute for Innovation and Improvement (2008) *Commissioning to make a bigger difference: A guide for NHS and social care commissioners on promoting service innovation*, London: DH.

Office for Disability Issues (2008) *Independent living: A cross-government strategy about independent living for disabled people*, London: HM Government Office for Disability Issues.

Poll, C. and Duffy, S. (eds) (2008) *A report on in Control's second phase: Evaluation and learning 2005–2007,* London: in Control publications, available at www.in-control.org.uk/dynamic_download/in_download_389.pdf

Poll, C. and others (2006) *A report on in Control's first phase 2003–2005,* London: in Control publications, available at www.library.nhs.uk/learningdisabilities/viewResource.aspx?resID=187216

Prime Minister's Strategy Unit (2005) *Improving the life chances of disabled people*, London: Cabinet Office.

Prime Minister's Strategy Unit (2007) *HM Government policy review: Building on progress: Public services*, London: HM Government.

Shaping Our Lives (2008) in General Social Care Council *Social work at its best: A statement of social work roles and tasks for the 21st century*, London: General Social Care Council.

Shaping Our Lives National User Network and others (2003) *Shaping our lives – from outset to outcome,* York: Joseph Rowntree Foundation.

Shaping Our Lives, National Centre for Independent Living and University of Leeds Centre for Disability Studies (2007) *SCIE people management knowledge review 17: Developing social care: Service users driving culture change*, London: SCIE.

Skills for Care (2007) *New type of worker/working*, available at www.skillsforcare.org.uk/view.asp?id=894

Skills for Care (2008) *News Release 30/06/08: Skills for Care launches first major study of direct payment employers and personal assistants*, Leeds: Skills for Care.

Taylor, J. and others (2007) *We are not stupid*, London: Shaping Our Lives and People First Lambeth.

TUC (Trades Union Congress) (2008) *Hard work, hidden lives: The short report on the commission on vulnerable employment*, London: TUC.

Image: 'Personalisation in social care –
some history and context' by Pen Mendonca
penmendonca@btinternet.com